What Our Readers Have Said...

"Although I consider myself a seasoned sales professional, it is helpful to have past learning's refreshed. The books were also beneficial because of the information concerning 'trends' in the sales relationship. The sales process should be viewed as dynamic since business relationships change regularly."

•

"For the particular business I am in and the type of sales calls I have, I find that the books in the Pinpoint Sales Training Series are very often applicable to how I conduct business. I would recommend them to other sales people, just not ones that are in my industry."

•

"These books provide very good concepts. It fits in well with the Bell Leadership training program that I attended in November."

•

"I use this material in these books and apply it to my customers and other employees I work with."

•

"I would like to know other topics. Is there anything on Production Management or Consultative Selling or Time Management?"

•

"These books are great tools that should be used as guidelines for our everyday

supervisory practices. You need to take the time to do a short self-evaluation when reading them."

•

"The Pinpoint Training Series delivers information that could be used in a lot different areas."

•

"I like this because I can take them with me to read at a convenient time. I feel the little time I have to spend in the office is best use on activities that directly relate to revenue opportunities. I like the short amount of time it takes to keep up with these."

•

"I prefer the self-study approach; it fits in with my schedule."

•

"My thought is that the real value of these books comes into effect when doing the action plans."

•

"Short and sweet. These books are easy to comprehend."

•

"I have enjoyed reading these books. They are relevant to today's work environment and the ongoing change in the way we manage our workforce."

•

"I do feel that these books have been very helpful to me at my job."

•

"I think a lot of the recommendations in these books are very useful, and can be applicable to everyday situations. If nothing else, it's a good reference guide to fall back upon if a situation arises in the future."

•

"These books are relevant to today's work environment and the ongoing change in the way we manage our workforce."

•

Cultivating a Competitive Advantage

Pinpoint Sales Skill Development Training Series

TIMOTHY F. BEDNARZ

MAJORIUM
BUSINESS PRESS

Pinpoint Sales Skill Development Training Series
"Cultivating a Competitive Advantage"
Timothy F. Bednarz

Graphic design: Monika Pawlak

Majorium Business Press
2025 Main Street
Stevens Point, WI 54481
715.342.1018 • 800.654.4935

ISBN 978-1-882181-95-7

Printed in the United States of America

Introduction

The Pinpoint Sales Skill Development Training Series is designed for targeted training and education regarding increased improvement in a specific skill or competency.

Each book within this series is designed to be easy to use, understand and apply to your job. It can be used as a basis for training individuals, as a discussion guide or as a personal training tool.

Each chapter within this book discusses a specific concept. When you have completed all eight chapters you should have a 360° perspective of the topic.

Additionally, each chapter is divided into specific sections:

- The first section provides you with an overview of the topic
- The Implications section discusses why the concept is important, and why it is important to learn and apply.
- The Strategies, Tips & Techniques to Apply section teaches how to use and apply the particular concept to your work.
- The Points to Ponder section gives you something to think about or to be discussed with a group setting. These are questions not meant to be immediately answered, but to be pondered over time.
- The Training Activity section provides you with the tools to transfer what you have learned to your job. It is designed to help create an action plan to effectively apply the concept.

Each of the topics in this series is time-tested and proven in the marketplace. They have been used by thousands of employees as training tools. Many of the users have commented that what made these books valuable, was the ability to refer to them when a problem surfaced. They indicated that they remembered reading about the exact problem. They referred back to these books and found an appropriate solution.

You will find them equally valuable as a resource in your professional development library.

Table of Contents

LEARNING OBJECTIVES:

- Appreciate the importance of understanding a customer's needs.
- Identify the consequences of failing to address the customer's needs.
- Understand how to prepare to identify a customer's needs.
- Understand how to properly probe for needs.
- Understand how to differentiate themselves.
- Determine how to properly qualify a prospect.
- Know if and when a prospect is properly qualified.
- Determine strategies to use to identify customer needs.
- Understand the value of effective questioning techniques.
- Apply effective listening to gather information.
- Effectively use questioning to advance the sale.
- Use questioning to establish commitment.
- Translate information into expertise.
- Understand the elements of product knowledge.

1

Effective Questioning Techniques

Effective questioning is the most basic tool salespeople have in their toolkit. It is indispensable for uncovering problems, building trust and credibility, and focusing customers on an effective solution; yet it is a skill that is often taken for granted.

Small details about customers can make a great deal of difference in the solutions salespeople offer. The problem is that many tend to interrogate rather than guide and direct a productive discussion by using probing questions with their customers.

It is often believed that effective questioning is the result of being internally intuitive rather than outwardly skillful. This assumption may have been true in the past, but with today's customers, it is essential to solve more complex problems. Along with the increasing complexities of problems, salespeople must deal with customers who are far more demanding than ever. To satisfy customers, salespeople must use effective questioning skills and approaches.

IMPLICATIONS — WHAT THIS MEANS TO YOU

Professional selling includes setting individual goals for effective questioning and applying the most beneficial methods of getting customers to open up and completely disclose problems, issues and expectations. Good questioning takes careful planning. Key outcomes must be defined, with activities to advance the sale structured and connected to the questioning process.

The questioning process must be used as a guide to create the best possible outcome. The key is to facilitate a productive atmosphere in which to meet customer expectations and generate ideas that lead to solutions. Questioning, interaction and imagination are the three major mediums used to bring it all together. Planning and utilizing the right techniques allows salespeople to communicate across barriers that would otherwise tend to hinder the process.

Information is the lifeblood of selling. Without specific and detailed information to effectively determine problems, concerns and needs, salespeople will undoubtedly face a number of stalls, objections and needless complications.

Salespeople need good questioning skills to:

- Gather information and facts that facilitate the best available solutions
- Develop information regarding their customers' viewpoints and feelings
- Confirm each customer's understanding of his or her problems
- Develop trust, credibility and rapport with their customers
- Uncover hidden agendas
- Move their customers toward a specific solution

This is important for salespeople to understand because many view asking their customers too many questions as obtrusive. Or, salespeople can simply feel it is not important to gather as much information as possible.

STRATEGIES, TIPS & TECHNIQUES TO APPLY

To successfully identify customers' needs and concerns, salespeople must be sure to explore the right areas with focused questions. A number of strategies and techniques will help salespeople improve their questioning skills:

Put the Customer at Ease

Individuals made to feel comfortable and at ease are more likely to share in-depth information. It is essential for customers to understand that their interests take precedence and that they are valued and important.

Ask Permission

Salespeople should never assume they have blanket permission to query a customer. It is always appropriate for them to get direct permission from the customer to ask questions. Such deference demonstrates the salesperson's sensitivity and gives the customer a sense of power and control over the process. It also greatly reduces the customer's fears and anxieties.

Word Questions Carefully

The way a question is worded can either build trust or turn a conversation into an interrogation that erodes trust. It is essential for salespeople to watch their manners and avoid words and a tone that may put a customer on the defensive.

As salespeople move from question to question, they should acknowledge the customer's responses before proceeding. These responses should convey genuine interest. Salespeople should avoid offering, "that's nice" and similar empty replies.

Start with Broad Questions

Salespeople should start the process with broad, open-ended questions. Beginning a conversation in this way puts the customer at ease.

Build on Responses

Salespeople should ask questions in a logical sequence. Doing so allows them to maintain a conversational tone when seeking certain responses. As the customer answers a question, salespeople should listen closely for key words and phrases, and focus each subsequent question in a way that allows the customer to elaborate.

Use Personal Expertise

Salespeople should use their experiences and expertise to frame and formulate questions. As they actively question the customer, salespeople can tie in previous experiences to help demonstrate their value.

Keep It Simple

Salespeople should keep questions simple and straightforward, as direct and useful questions result in useful information. They should avoid complicated multipart questions that distract the customer from the focus of the conversation.

Listen

Salespeople should step back from the conversation as quickly as possible and allow the customer to talk. They need to listen and carefully analyze the discussion points, comments and responses.

Don't Interrogate and Intimidate

Instead of leading a discussion focused on a specific issue or problem, many salespeople tend to interrogate customers. Interrogation puts customers on the defensive and instills in them the desire to end the meeting as quickly as possible.

Keep Questions Focused

Salespeople should lead customers through a discussion of specific problems, needs and concerns. Their questions must focus the conversation on the exact purpose of the desired outcome.

Respect Their Time

While customers are generally willing to give salespeople the time they need to develop information that will benefit both parties, most are extremely busy. Salespeople should respect time constraints and limit their questioning to the primary focus of their call—to obtain the specific information they need to work out a favorable solution as quickly as possible.

Use Seven Questioning Techniques

The following seven questioning techniques work to eliminate barriers to meeting customer expectations and solving their problems quickly and courteously:

Know Something About the Customer – Salespeople should begin the questioning process by learning as much as they can up front about the particular customers they are dealing with. They need to determine and stay within the boundaries defining the customer's problem or situation as well as get a sense of the rules they are playing by and their expectations. This technique works well to eliminate multiple problems that can surface and slow the sales process.

Monitor Vocabulary – Salespeople should be on the watch for slang, jargon or idioms that can muddy their message. Professional questions are planned, clear, short and to the point. When constructed in this way, they yield usable information. The use of inappropriate terms conveys a lack of professionalism, confuses customers and lengthens the sales process.

Soften Tone – Salespeople need to maintain a soft voice when talking with customers. Tending to want to talk louder—especially over the phone when they have trouble understanding something or when emotions are raised—salespeople need to realize that a loud voice can mean different things to different customers. Many customers resent being treated as though they are hearing impaired when they are only trying to carefully comprehend or interpret what is being said. Others react negatively to a loud voice because they feel the salesperson is talking down to them.

Speak Calmly, Slowly and Clearly – Salespeople should make sure that the most important questions are communicated in a calm, clear and concise manner and at a slower-than-normal speed. As customers are already prone to losing interest in a presentation when they are attempting to gather certain pieces of information, hasty salespeople will further hinder the process. When customers are exposed to fast-paced questioning and shifts in subjects, barriers are often created and meanings and interpretations confused and lost. Good salespeople give individuals every chance to hear and interpret their words and phrases so that customers gain meaning from the questioning process.

Make It a Point to Repeat – If a customer asks to have a question repeated for clarity or understanding, it is important for the salesperson not to change the wording or add anything when replying. They must answer using the same inflections, tone and words.

Most salespeople want to say, "let me put it another way," when in fact the customer is focused on most of the words spoken the first time around and only wants to clarify others that were missed. When the question is altered, it ends up getting lost in translation and adding to the confusion of the questioning process.

Encourage Questions – As part of the problem solving process, salespeople need to be open and do everything in their power to encourage customers to ask more questions. Because customers are often hesitant to display confusion or ignorance about what was said or asked, salespeople should urge them to ask questions anytime they wish to do so, and make certain to treat them with respect and dignity when they do. Absent these reassurances, shy customers may never ask a question, leading them to put off a decision to purchase.

Facilitate and Reinforce Communication and Questioning – Salespeople should plan the endings to the inquiry process, as well as any subsequent conversations. A sales encounter should never end abruptly. Instead, the skillful approach is to take the time to summarize important points covered throughout the process. Summing up critical points, issues, facts and data slowly and clearly helps prevent misinterpretations. By going over what was said, addressed and developed, salespeople will also convey friendliness, patience and the value of the customer.

POINTS TO PONDER — SOMETHING TO THINK ABOUT

1. Do you do everything possible to encourage your customers to ask questions in regard to issues and concerns that arise during an inquiry process?
2. Do you make it a point to repeat important data, information or questions in order to make them clearly understood?
3. How do you show your customers that you genuinely care about them through your questioning? Explain.
4. Do you overcome stalls, objections and resistance by getting your customers to relax and open up?

TRAINING ACTIVITY — APPLICATION & ACTION PLAN

Develop a series of questions that will focus a customer on the immediate goal you set for the appointment.

- The ideal way to do this is to focus on a particular prospect and develop specific questions that relate to him or her.
- Questions can then be adapted to meet the needs of similar prospects.

2

Probing Questions That Completely Identify Problems and Issues

When salespeople uncover their customers' real needs, they are presented with a wealth of information that they often do not know what to do with. Salespeople know that they have to identify needs, but will typically select one or two favorite facts upon which to build their presentation and ignore the rest of the information.

The first step to uncovering a customer's needs is to sit down and have a conversation with them: not to sell them, but to simply talk about their business. As basic as this seems, it is a very difficult discussion for many salespeople to engage in, as it takes time, appears to accomplish little if anything and keeps them from what they consider to be their primary sales activity.

IMPLICATIONS — WHAT THIS MEANS TO YOU

When salespeople first meet with a customer, they have a unique opportunity to learn about their business, organizational environment and all of the elements defining their "universe." This requires taking the time to sit down and have a conversation with the prospect—an essential and often overlooked activity.

Failing to engage in such a fact-finding discussion can undermine the sales process and possibly the sale itself. As this stage provides the first and most significant opportunity to get to personally know the customer and create a positive impression, salespeople should not underestimate its importance.

It should be noted that there is a difference between knowledge and information. Unfortunately, most salespeople will collect information about a customer's needs without converting it into usable knowledge.

When salespeople take the information they have collected and apply their experience and expertise to it, they have the ability to convert it into knowledge that can give them the competitive advantage. This is because most customers are not aware of the opportunities and possibilities that a company, product or service can provide to them. Indeed, many are completely unaware of their essential product requirements until after the fact.

Through the proper application of knowledge and expertise, salespeople can provide a genuine service to their customers and help them make an informed and qualified buying decision.

STRATEGIES, TIPS & TECHNIQUES TO APPLY

When salespeople take the time to converse with rather than solely sell their customers, several things occur that are critical to the success of the sale:

1. They get the customer to talk and lower their defenses.
2. They loosen the customer up to talk more and reveal more about his or her business.
3. They develop trust and rapport.
4. They may discover an item of importance that the competition was unable to find.

The initial conversation should focus on uncovering basic information about the current situation. Salespeople can do this through the use of open-ended questions, which are crucial for establishing trust.

People like to talk about themselves and their business. The more they talk, the more they will like the salesperson and think they are adept conversationalists.

Salespeople will often have difficulty refraining from presenting everything they know about the customer's business. This puts the prospect on the defensive—people don't like "know-it-alls." Even if the salesperson is correct in everything they say, the customer will not trust them or want to do business with them.

Thus the customer should be doing all of the talking. Salespeople should apply their knowledge and expertise of the customer's business to developing open-ended and probing questions.

During this initial discussion, salespeople should avoid discussing the customer's problems. If they do, they will immediately place them on the defensive and force them to lie about their current situation. Rather than focus on problems, the salesperson should put the customer at ease to earn their trust.

When problems are discussed, many salespeople will impatiently focus on the first problem revealed, not allowing the customer to fully explain the extent of their situation. This is often counterproductive, as research has shown that many prospects will not take action until they air three or more significant problems.

As salespeople continue to ask questions, they should use their three or four product strengths as the basis of their inquiry. This effectively positions their product or service as a potential solution by making the customer think that the idea to want those product strengths was their own. The salesperson's job is to create a desire for that which he or she is selling. Open-ended, probing questions built around a product's strengths effectively accomplishes this.

The final aspect of this initial conversation is for the salesperson to create as many options for the customer as possible. The more alternatives and options that can be created, the greater the salesperson's odds of getting the sale.

Salespeople should understand that there are specific purposes and goals behind their questioning, including:

Objectives

One of the salesperson's primary goals is to clearly define what the customer wants to accomplish. It is surprising how many salespeople ignore this basic task and move on to sell what they feel the customer wants and needs.

When salespeople uncover specific needs by identifying the changes that the customer's business is undergoing and the areas of pain and discontent with existing suppliers, they are ultimately able to identify what the customer wants to accomplish. A clear identification of customer needs pinpoints what their objective is.

The common reaction is, "Why don't I just ask what they want to accomplish?" The answer is that until a salesperson takes the time to identify these issues, individual customers may not know what they want to accomplish, often because they are unaware of what is possible or the options available to them.

Requirements

Salespeople must identify the customer's requirements. These are the items that the customer "must have" and that drive the need for a solution. If a salesperson is unable to identify these factors, it is unlikely that they will be able to fully satisfy the customer after the sale.

Since many prospects are unaware of the options available to them and base the majority of their decisions on past experiences, they may not be aware of the requirements they need to receive a fully effective solution and to be fully satisfied with their purchase. Consequently, it is up to the salesperson to discuss the prospect's requirements and identify the elements that they have to have as part of their solution.

Refinement

When salespeople uncover a prospect's needs, they have the ability to refine their objectives and make them more precise. Often prospects are not aware of specific ways that they can improve their operations and effectiveness with the salesperson's products and services.

Every company and product has unique capabilities. Salespeople often fail to leverage these capabilities—which can often solve a number of potential problems—to their advantage.

Salespeople need to focus on the prospect's needs—not their products. In this way they can refine the prospect's need in a manner that creates a desire for their unique capabilities. Successfully done, this creates a strong competitive advantage.

Identify Add-Ons

Beyond the customer's requirements, or "must-haves," most have a series of add-ons, or "nice-to-haves." These are other features and capabilities that they would like to see added to their purchase.

Salespeople must take the time to identify and rank these additional criteria before the customer has the opportunity to explore other competitors. The success of the sale will depend on how the customer's criteria are ranked. The salesperson's goal is to create the best match between their product's strengths and the customer's criteria. The first salesperson in the door has the ability to greatly influence the customer. Properly done, the competition will find it difficult to compete with the refined and polished criteria.

Compelling Reason

After the salesperson has refined the customer's needs and criteria, it is important to give the customer a compelling reason to buy their product or service. *Inc. Magazine* reported that one of the major causes of lost sales and failed businesses is the failure to provide customers with a compelling reason to switch from their existing vendor.

The salesperson who has taken a customer this far must conclude their analysis with a compelling reason to switch, otherwise they are leaving the door open for competitors to take advantage of their hard work.

POINTS TO PONDER — SOMETHING TO THINK ABOUT

1. What is your initial approach when first meeting with a prospect? Is it a discussion or a presentation?
2. What techniques do you use to get the prospect to talk and lower his or her defenses?
3. How are you able to apply and use customer knowledge to your advantage?
4. How well do you refine a customer's needs to your competitive advantage?

TRAINING ACTIVITY — APPLICATION & ACTION PLAN

Develop a compelling reason why your prospects should switch from their existing suppliers to you.

1. Start with a rough draft or outline of your reasons.
2. Refine and polish by adding and deleting thoughts and reasons.
3. Create a final draft that is clear and concise.
4. Finalize it into a statement that you can use.

3

Factors That Impact Qualifying a Sale

Salespeople have an obligation to sell a customer if a need exists and they have the ability to make a purchase. Often salespeople feel that once they have established those two facts, their responsibility to further qualify the customer ends. However qualifying entails a number of other factors that ultimately impact the salesperson's success or failure with the customer.

The time invested in properly qualifying a prospect has a strong return on investment for the salesperson who makes the effort to do so. While many attempt to short-circuit the process, a properly qualified prospect can be sold more easily and in a shorter period of time.

IMPLICATIONS — WHAT THIS MEANS TO YOU

A properly qualified prospect should provide salespeople with the knowledge and information they need to determine the viability of their business as a customer, including the time and effort that will likely be needed to sell them and whether a legitimate sales opportunity exists. The salesperson's goal is to identify as much of the customer's information and criteria as possible before investing the time and resources in selling them.

It is important for salespeople to understand that selling is not a game to be won or lost. It is a serious attempt to produce sales and revenues for their company. A salesperson cannot properly accomplish this task without the information to analyze and assess the customer's business and identify their true potential as legitimate sales opportunities. Without this information, salespeople will likely waste significant time and resources on poor sales candidates.

Sales are becoming increasingly complex—even when the salesperson is selling a relatively simple item. Buying decisions that were once made by a single decision maker are now the responsibility of a buying committee. Increased buying channels and product options have rendered product evaluation more time-consuming and complicated. Buyers are more highly trained and sophisticated. Consequently, the sale of a product or service can consume a great deal of the salesperson's time and resources.

Salespeople are not paid to sell but to generate sales and revenue. In this regard, qualifying becomes an aspect of time and resource management. When salespeople properly qualify a customer, they are identifying where to apply their resources to obtain the best return on their investment.

STRATEGIES, TIPS & TECHNIQUES TO APPLY

Salespeople are the facilitators of change. The process of selling involves convincing customers to make changes that can have an impact on their business. An essential part of selling, establishing rapport and building trust reduces the level of risk in the customer's mind in order to minimize their resistance to change. Consequently, the higher the levels of perceived risk and resistance to change, the longer the entire sales process will take.

As a time and resource management issue, salespeople must be cognizant of these factors. Since they are often under pressure to produce results, they must balance their efforts between customers with relatively low resistance to change and those with higher levels who may take longer to fully develop to the point of commitment. (Larger and more lucrative customers typically fall into this category.) Salespeople often create problems for themselves when they invest heavily in high-resistance customers due to their size and desirability. The intense investment takes away from their ability to meet short-term goals and quotas.

As salespeople proceed through the qualification process, there are three factors that they must accurately assess in identifying the desirability of a customer. These are:

Motivation

Customers may feel that there is nothing wrong with their existing vendor. They may not be motivated to change unless the benefits far outweigh the costs associated with change. This is the very reason that salespeople are taught to look for signs of pain or discontent with their existing suppliers. These signs identify the customer's motivation to change. They have identified areas that if improved may induce them to make a change.

Determination

Even if motivated, a customer may not have the will or power to ensure that a change will occur. The political atmosphere within the company or other factors may make internal changes difficult if not impossible. Consequently, a lack of personal determination can result in additional resistance to change. While this can be overcome, it will take salespeople additional time and resources to facilitate sufficient internal change to reduce risks and commit the customer to the sale.

Willingness

The final aspect of facilitating change with a customer is addressing whether it is worth the time and effort they will have to invest in switching to a new product or service. Installation, training and the learning curve for successful product implementation all impact the customer's overall motivation.

The customer's willingness to change can be tainted by previous bad experiences with other vendors, where problems and delays occurred. These negative experiences can sour the customer on everything related to the change. These issues can be resolved once they are uncovered by the salesperson, but it will take additional time to reduce the risk in the customer's mind.

Ultimately, the failure of the salesperson to identify these three qualifying factors will impact their overall results, and also provide the undercurrents that result in stalls and objections as prospects are compelled to deal with these issues.

The following factors should be considered the basis for a qualified customer.

Description of Problem or Need

Salespeople must be careful in defining or describing a customer's need or problem. As simple as it seems, faulty assumptions at this stage will taint the entire sales process. Rather, salespeople should have the customer define their own need or problem. When customers are unable to do this, salespeople should use a series of probing questions to help them identify their problems or needs. Salespeople should paraphrase and combine responses to ensure they understand what it is the customer needs resolved or addressed.

Level of Discontent

The level of discontent with existing circumstances must be clearly defined and understood by the customer. Additionally, the salesperson must be able to engage the customer in a meaningful two-way dialogue about key issues surrounding their problems. Salespeople who are unable to do this will find it difficult to sell the customer.

Prospect's Knowledge of Solution

Customers should have knowledge of a meaningful solution to their problems. The solution might not initially be product-specific, but it should define in the customer's mind what would be possible, if not ideal.

Champions

Each change or solution requires senior-level people to champion the change throughout the company. A failure to do so indicates that the seriousness of the problem is not being addressed at the appropriate levels of responsibility. If the salesperson does not identify a champion, changes will not occur.

Motivation

The salesperson needs to identify the specific and compelling factors motivating the prospect to seek a change and initiate the sales process. A lack of identifiable motivation can considerably lengthen the sales process.

Consequences

Customers should be aware of the consequences associated with their choice to change or not to change their current circumstances. Salespeople should be able to quantify these into financial terms the customer can readily understand.

Additionally, salespeople should quantify the cost of opportunity lost if the customer delays or postpones a buying decision, as these are consequences that the customer should consider.

Current Situation

Salespeople should have the facts and data to clearly identify the customer's current situation, including the existing products or services and related costs. This allows them to develop a comparison of their solutions and costs including implementation and any other associated costs to change.

Budget

Many customers will refuse to share their budget with salespeople for several reasons:

- Fear of being taken advantage of by the salesperson.
- Lack of a budget.
- Using the salesperson to develop prices to leverage a competitor with.
- Testing the market.

As each of these reasons has its own ramifications, salespeople must identify the basis for their customer's lack of candor.

Alternatives

Many sales remain unresolved with a decision not being made because the customer was prepared to live with the consequences, had something else in mind or found that the risks associated with change outweighed the benefits. In other instances, customers may have no intention of buying, using a competitor to leverage the other to get a better deal.

Evaluation

Salespeople should be aware of the criteria and standards that will be used to evaluate a product or service for selection. Additionally, they should be informed of the specific results of the evaluation and how their product or service was rated against others.

Implementation

It is a good idea for salespeople to inquire as to the customer's plans to implement a product change in order to determine how far in advance he or she is thinking. This also provides insight into what and how they are thinking about the use and application of the product or service.

Expectations

Salespeople should be aware of the customer's expectations of what switching to their product or service will mean to their business. Faulty or exaggerated expectations can result in problems during and after the sale.

POINTS TO PONDER — SOMETHING TO THINK ABOUT

1. Have you had a situation where you thought the sale was final only to lose it for no apparent reason?
2. Have you considered a customer's motivation to change as you qualify them?
3. How extensively do you qualify your customers? Is the process more, or less intensive than described above?
4. What qualifying criteria do you consider important?

TRAINING ACTIVITY — APPLICATION & ACTION PLAN

Make a list of the customers that you are currently working on.

1. Evaluate each according to their motivation, determination and willingness to change.
2. Rate each factor on a scale of one to ten, ten being the highest.
3. Prioritize your customers according to their scores.
4. Compare and contrast this list with your own prioritized list. This should show you where to invest your time and resources first.

4

Key Value Indicators

Many salespeople get tangled up in price objections and other factors that tend to muddy the waters rather than clearly present the advantages of their offering. While some hold that buyers are concerned more with price than results, market research demonstrates that for most products, factors other than price rank significantly higher. Buyers are still looking for the best deal, but are more interested in value and results.

The salesperson's competitive edge lies in the total value they can communicate for their products and services. This is the package of expectations created during the sales process. A deal can still be negotiated when the competition has 10 advantages over the salesperson's product—if they can offer the one result that is most important to the customer.

IMPLICATIONS – WHAT THIS MEANS TO YOU

Customers compare products one-to-one against the competition—not one-to-one against the world. Every product doesn't have the same total value the salesperson's product has. The uniqueness of their product goes well beyond the details to the promise of satisfaction. The key lies in knowing what is of value to each customer. It's not the product, but what representatives put into their product—the way they link it to what customers want—that gives them the edge. Selling from the customer's viewpoint is the building block of buyer motivation.

The value of any given product can also include how unique it is, how badly the customer is in need of it, what it would cost them to replace it and precedents that speak to its high value. If the customer has a significant problem that the salesperson's product will address, the value of their offering increases substantially.

STRATEGIES, TIPS & TECHNIQUES TO APPLY

In order to specifically identify their product's strengths, salespeople should select the product or service they are most interested in selling more of and compare it directly to their competitor's products using the following key value categories. Products should be analyzed according to at least one advantage they have over the competition and the benefit(s) this provides to the customer.

Financial Differences – Price rates, charges or incentives to buy.

Convenience – Location, hours, time efficiency, self-service, toll-free help lines, or the fact that service personnel will call on the buyer.

Personal Attention – Frequent contact, consulting, relationship management or other services provided by the salesperson.

Information – Easy access to account data, product specialists, financial information, statements, reports, newsletters and seminars.

Service Quality – Speed, accuracy, responsiveness, waiting time, cleanliness or an attention to detail.

Security – Insurance, guarantees, warrantees or security ensuring privacy.

Emotional Satisfaction – Prestige, sense of belonging, customer relationship, familiarity and recognition.

Product – Availability, selection, innovation, or special products and services designed to meet specific needs.

Decision Making – Ability to make quick decisions regarding resolution of customer problems, approvals on orders and specifications, contract release and overall flexibility.

Customer Support – Training and education, sales support, co-op advertising, warehousing, distribution and product servicing.

Contract Terms – Payment plans and product minimums.

Technical Superiority – Systems, automation, product durability, innovation and reliability.

Financial Impact – Cost savings, productivity gains and return on investment.

These and any other additional factors comprise the total value of the salesperson's product or service. The more factors salespeople can identify, the higher the value of their product, with any one factor alone potentially making the difference to the customer.

POINTS TO PONDER — SOMETHING TO THINK ABOUT

1. Do you present your products using key value indicators that identify the advantages they provide to your customer?
2. What additional key value indicators would apply to your products? Explain.

TRAINING ACTIVITY — APPLICATION & ACTION PLAN

1. Select the product or service you're most interested in selling more of and compare it directly to your competitor's products using the above key value categories.
2. Analyze your product by identifying at least one advantage you have over the competition and one benefit this provides to the customer.

5

Strategies to Uncover a Customer's Needs

Effective questioning techniques enable salespeople to efficiently guide their customers through a polished sequence of inquiries. They should not interrogate in their application, but persuade customers to respond rationally and thoroughly. The questioning process should be structured to provide detailed information to effectively help identify acceptable solutions.

All sales questioning has three inherent functions: gathering, developing and interpreting in-depth information. Some questioning techniques are better suited to obtaining the particular facts, data and input needed to solve customer problems in a fast and friendly manner. Salespeople need to be aware of the most effective approaches and how to use them to their advantage.

Effective listening and questioning skills are closely linked. Questioning becomes worthless without the ability to clearly hear and precisely interpret what customers have to say. Salespeople must also be attuned to multiple levels of listening, as each ultimately impacts how they respond to their customers and their subsequent relationships with them.

IMPLICATIONS — WHAT THIS MEANS TO YOU

Effective questioning techniques are used to facilitate the communication of information and solutions between the salesperson and customer. Many sales problems stem from faulty communication in which the cause of a problem or issue is not clearly comprehended and understood. Because this results in a failure to identify symptoms, faulty solutions are then presented, which lead to more callbacks and intervention procedures.

It is essential for salespeople to appreciate that, when viewed over the long-term, it takes little additional time and effort to effectively resolve a problem or issue the first time, even when multiple calls or the cooperation of others within the company are involved. In reality, it takes more time to go back and rework the process when a sales problem is mishandled due to ineffective communication and inadequate questioning techniques.

Absent the development of sufficient information, salespeople cannot efficiently attend to their customers' needs in order to meet or exceed their expectations. This is why good questioning techniques are key to successful sales encounter outcomes. Becoming versed in the advantages and disadvantages of each type of customer questioning allows salespeople to make appropriate choices as to how, where and when to ask for input. The purpose of effective questioning is to produce a customer friendly atmosphere so that it becomes easier to obtain what is needed to formulate a satisfactory solution.

By blending three types of specific questioning techniques, information can be obtained in an efficient, non-threatening manner. Because of it, customers are not offended or intimidated by the steady "drilling" that normally accompanies the information-gathering process. Salespeople need to remember that their questions must be designed primarily to help clarify problems and issues in a structured, concise and clear manner.

Listening is a critical sales skill that goes beyond passively absorbing what customers are saying to include "reading between the lines," carefully analyzing what is being communicated, and determining how to craft the most effective solution. It implies actively replying to what customers are saying with a well thought-out response, as many salespeople will ignore what has been said to them in order to state what they feel must be said. This leads to a disconnect with little or no real communication taking place between parties.

It is important for salespeople to pose specific questions to customers, and then get out of the way of their answers. Clients should be allowed to speak without interruption in order to provide vital information. Salespeople need to interject more probing questions only to arrive at the heart of an unclear or possibly misinterpreted issue or thought.

STRATEGIES, TIPS & TECHNIQUES TO APPLY

People like talking about themselves. Salespeople who dominate conversations generally feel they have done a good job of communicating, reacting, and conveying professionalism. However, customers feel just the opposite, and are more often than not frustrated by the process.

With this in mind, salespeople should be aware of five levels of listening. The first three completely undermine their professional stance as a good listener, while the remainder can greatly improve the customer inquiry and discussion process. Each affects the outcome of conversations, dialogues and the customer relationship building process. These are:

Preoccupied

At this level, salespeople are distracted listeners. They're concentrating on their notes, gathering information to impart to their customers, or allowing their minds to wander onto something else. Because they are not listening specifically to what is being said, they lose valuable information and input. This leaves customers with the impression that what they are saying is not important, nor is the business the company and its representative say they want.

Feigned

On the feigned level—the most common level of detrimental listening—salespeople pretend to hear what their customers are saying. They tend to look attentive, and make the appropriate motions and sounds that indicate they are following along, but are actually thinking about what they are going to say next and not listening at all.

As salespeople only pretending to listen will often respond with a wholly unrelated message or thought, they lose credibility in the eyes of the customer. While they may feel they made an appropriate reply, they did not respond with what their customers wanted to hear. Incomplete, muddied or "off-the-wall" responses openly demonstrate a lack of respect, and undermine the ability to build an atmosphere of trust. Customers begin to feel insulted, belittled, and unimportant.

Selective

Salespeople operating on a selective listening level develop faulty perceptions and understandings of their customers' needs. Even though they are listening carefully and reacting appropriately, they allow their biases and preconceived notions to filter out key aspects of what is being said, which leads to misinterpreting specific messages or points. Their determining what is relevant and important limits what they actively ask and learn, which in turn leads to poorly crafted solutions.

Attentive

In the attentive listening level, salespeople are able to demonstrate their listening skills and ability to hear. They do this by paraphrasing and actively responding to what is being said with replies directly reflecting their customers' comments and concerns. However, at this level, salespeople need to guard against becoming emotionally aloof throughout the discussion and inquiry process. A facade of emotional connection may be created, but salespeople who attempt to listen attentively can easily get distracted, which leads to becoming emotionally disconnected from their customers and surrounding circumstances.

Empathetic

Emotionally invested in the conversations, salespeople are able to "think outside of the box" and view situations from their customers' perspective. They are genuinely concerned about their customers' problems and concerns, and react passionately to them.

When customers have their concerns treated as the salesperson's top priority, they feel they are genuinely cared about, and immediately become interested in developing long-term relationships with the salesperson and their company.

Employing Specific Types of Questions

Salespeople should have a full understanding of the following three types of questioning that work to develop in-depth information. Each type of questioning plays an important role in the sales process and is a tool that skilled salespeople should consistently apply in all their encounters.

Closed-Ended Questions – Closed-ended questions are questions that allow customers to provide a limited response, typically a "yes" or "no." While these questions are restrictive in nature, there are distinct advantages and disadvantages to their use:

Advantages

- Closed-ended questions are quick and require little time investment, just the short answer;
- Provide the salesperson with a high level of control over the customer contact;
- Can be used to obtain direct and specific answers.

Disadvantages

- Incomplete answers require the salesperson to get more information from the customer;
- Closed-ended questions can be leading, resulting in inaccurate assumptions and conclusions;
- Discourage the customer from openly disclosing information;
- Can irritate the customer by making them feel interrogated.

Content Questions – Content questions are familiar "Who, What, Where, When and How" questions. Comprising the salesperson's primary tool, these will effectively develop details and explanations of the problem with the customer.

Advantages

- Content questions are easy and natural for salespeople to use;
- Obtain the facts and information related to the problem;

- Are familiar and comfortable for customers and salespeople to ask.

Disadvantages

- Content questions may not get to the underlying issues;
- Will rarely elicit customers' true feelings and emotions;
- May cause salespeople to miss key non-technical issues and concerns.

Open-Ended Questions – Open-ended questions allow salespeople to solicit additional information from their customers. They invite customers to talk about the problem, while establishing rapport, gathering information and increasing understanding. More importantly they do not lead the customer.

Advantages

- Open-ended questions develop trust;
- Are perceived as less threatening by the customer;
- Allow for a greater freedom of expression;
- Probe for the issue's context;
- Measure the customer's understanding of a problem.

Disadvantages

- Open-ended questions can be time-consuming, as customers may be long-winded in their responses;
- Can generate superfluous and irrelevant information;
- May result in the customer needing to focus their answers.

Additionally, there is a series and sequence of questions salespeople can employ to fully understand the extent and seriousness of a particular customer's problem. These include:

History Questions – The purpose of history questions is to gather information regarding background, circumstances and other pertinent facts surrounding the customer's problem. Salespeople can use these questions to verify information that they know or suspect to be the case:

- What is the problem?
- How long has it been happening?
- When did the problem start?
- How long was the product or service being used before the problem started?

Symptom Questions – Although a common service pitfall is to address symptoms instead of the core issue—resulting in a recurring problem and further callbacks—symptom questions will provide the salesperson an effective way to have the customer fully describe their problem. Symptom questions include:

- Describe exactly what is happening.
- How would you describe ____?
- What do you observe when the problem occurs?

Cause Questions – The purpose of the cause question is to determine the specific origins of symptoms. This allows salespeople to probe more deeply into the problem and attempt to pinpoint the root cause. These questions allow salespeople to make an assessment of the problem and should trigger specific remedial actions:

- Do you have any idea what may be causing that?
- What factors bring about the problem?
- What are you doing when the problem begins?
- Does the product or service display any codes or messages?

Complication Questions – Complication questions determine the seriousness of the customer's problem and the impact it is having on their job and business. These questions should indicate to the salesperson the priority the problem should take:

- How does that affect ____?
- What does the problem lead to?
- What will happen if the problem is not immediately addressed?

- What additional problems does this create for you?

Cure Questions – As not all solutions are considered equal in the customer's eyes, it is important to determine what they perceive to be a fair solution with cure questions. In many cases, a customer's solution is far less demanding than what the salesperson's company was willing to provide. Sample questions include:

- What do you want us to do?
- What would you consider an acceptable solution?
- If we did _____, would you consider that to be an acceptable solution?

Salespeople must learn to blend these questions into a smooth and polished sequence that both delineates the problem and points to an acceptable solution. It is not enough to ask three or four history questions and then move on to three or four symptom questions and so on. Rather, they should develop a logical, smooth, and conversational flow to their questioning that doesn't interrogate customers, but elicits information about their problem.

POINTS TO PONDER — SOMETHING TO THINK ABOUT

1. While everyone falls into every listening level listed above at one time or another, what level(s) of listening do you normally apply during an average customer call or contact? Explain.
2. How effectively do you blend the three different styles of questioning into your sales encounters?
3. Do you use one style of questioning more often than the others? If so, why?
4. Does your current approach effectively move the customer through a logical sequence in order to gather information and develop solutions, or is it more random in nature?

TRAINING ACTIVITY — APPLICATION & ACTION PLAN

1. Create three or four questions in each of the following categories:
    a. History
    b. Symptom
    c. Cause
    d. Complication
    e. Cure
2. Select one or two questions from each category.
3. Develop a polished and effective sequence of questions that leads the customer through all of the various questioning categories.
4. Use these questions with customers. Revise them until you are able to question customers in a polished and conversational manner.

6

Developing Customer Knowledge

Salespeople must ask themselves how well they really understand their customers. It's a simple question that is often the subject of banter in the office, but how many salespeople really develop a complete understanding of their customers? Salespeople are often too busy getting to the next sale before they fully understand what the customer really wants from them.

IMPLICATIONS — WHAT THIS MEANS TO YOU

Fortunately or unfortunately, depending upon one's perspective, customers are putting their foot down and saying, "Enough!" Whether salespeople like it or not, the days of traditional hit-and-run selling are over. As customers become more sophisticated, they demand more sophistication from the vendors servicing their needs.

Salespeople who completely understand the needs of their customers and are able to meet those needs with their products and services are the ones getting the sale. Conversely, salespeople who still employ manipulative sales tactics are experiencing difficulty making their numbers. The customer has changed, and salespeople must adapt their selling techniques to these changing needs.

Salespeople who wish to develop a comprehensive understanding of their customers' needs must conduct a needs assessment. Parameters to be included in this assessment are discussed below.

What Are the Customer's Needs?

It is the responsibility of salespeople to assess the customer's real needs. While the potential buyer may assist in identifying these, it is the role of the salesperson to probe for hidden or unknown needs. Persistent questioning is the starting point for determining these obscured concerns. Some customers know exactly what they want and need; others don't. It's up to the salesperson to sift through the information.

What Are the Problems?

The problems the customer is facing are early indicators of their needs. Problems often create a sense of urgency in the potential buyer to change the way they do business. When salespeople determine the problems that a customer is facing, they can begin to fashion unique solutions based upon their products or services.

What Are the Opportunities?

Opportunities are assessed by visiting the customer and by talking with buyers, users, and anyone involved with the salesperson's product. These interviews often paint a complete picture of the present environment and the opportunities that are available to the salesperson. It's up to salespeople to visit, talk, observe and listen; the opportunities that one discovers can be surprising.

Are There Any Limitations?

The limitations on a specific sale can take many forms. Salespeople must work within budgets and time frames and cope with facility and operational restrictions. All sales have some form of limitation that affects how a product can solve the prospective buyer's problem. It's up to the salesperson to identify these limitations and determine how to work around them.

Who Is the Decision Maker and Actual User of the Product?

Salespeople are often dealing with mid-level managers or purchasing agents during most of the selling process. These people are responsible for screening information for the buyer or decision maker. Whenever possible, it is important to talk with the actual decision maker, as it will shorten the sales cycle and smooth the process.

Additionally, someone other than the actual buyer often uses the product that is being sold. It is important for salespeople to gather feedback from the users of the product because they often have direct though unapparent input into the sales process. By dealing directly with the actual users, it minimizes the risk of salespeople being blindsided.

Questions to address when dealing with these behind-the-scenes constituencies include:

> *What Are They Seeking from the Salesperson?* – Since these are often hidden groups, unless salespeople have initiated direct contact, they will not be able to determine specific needs. Additionally, the screener may not have a real grasp of the details and information needed to discuss the issue with the salesperson. To determine the company's actual needs and agendas, salespeople need to meet with the people directly involved with the product or service.
>
> *What Are They Expecting from the Salesperson's Product?* – Meeting expectations is critical to the long-term success of a relationship with a potential buyer. The screener may have no idea of the expectations of the decision maker or the final customer. They might be able to furnish screening specifications, but it is up to the salesperson to determine the actual expectations of the sub-groups who control the buying process.
>
> *What Are the Salesperson's Solutions?* – Once salespeople have discovered the customer's actual needs and expectations, they are able to craft a solution based on the corresponding requirements. Lacking

this critical information, all a salesperson is able to do is meet general specifications and quote a price that will often be evaluated in an unfavorable light.

How Does the Salesperson's Solution Meet Expectations? – It is critical that the salesperson's solution be fashioned to meet the expectations of the actual constituencies responsible for the buying decision. The more closely salespeople are able to craft their solution to meet these expectations, the more favorably it positions them and negates the pure bidding process that was the original preference of the prospect or customer.

POINTS TO PONDER — SOMETHING TO THINK ABOUT

1. How complete is your own understanding of the individual customers that you serve? Explain.
2. Do you take the time to develop a complete understanding of their wants or needs, or do you just attempt to sell what you think they need?.

TRAINING ACTIVITY — APPLICATION & ACTION PLAN

Select a customer that you are currently working with.

1. Using the questions listed above in this lesson, develop a comprehensive needs analysis.
2. Based upon your findings, determine how this information alters your initial sales approach.

7

What Customers Need to Know

Informational requirements tend to vary from situation to situation. Some customers may require high levels of information, while others only minimal amounts. It is imperative for salespeople to understand how to balance the information they present in order to meet individual customers' specific product or service-related issues and concerns, as well as their interrelated informational requirements.

When viewing the scope of proper customer education, it is far too easy for salespeople to stumble into common problems and pitfalls as they attempt to short-circuit the sales process in order to push the sale and earn a commission. The majority of sales problems stem directly from a failure to properly qualify individual customers and supply them with insightful, in-depth education. These two areas are extremely important within the sales process.

IMPLICATIONS — WHAT THIS MEANS TO YOU

Many salespeople have the tendency to overburden their customers with too much information that is often not thoroughly read, understood or applied—then quickly forgotten or discarded. Conversely, some salespeople provide too little information, which leads to uninformed buying decisions. Salespeople must not assume individual customers are all the same, and be certain to identify the informational needs for each.

Customers' informational needs must be completely understood before messages, discussions and materials can be properly balanced. This is essential for providing the right information at the appropriate time in order to help customers make more suitable and customized purchasing decisions.

Numerous problems occur when salespeople fail to both adequately educate their customers as to their product's specific value and differentiate them from those of the competition. These include being brushed off or stalled later in the sales process and encountering numerous objections, especially toward the close. These problems can result in lost sales.

Supplying customers with adequate knowledge and education is vital to overall success. Without being thoroughly educated and informed as to the value that particular products or services offer, customers will most often assume a default position, which is to judge all of them as similar and evaluate them on the basis of price alone. This is a problem that salespeople can readily overcome.

STRATEGIES, TIPS & TECHNIQUES TO APPLY

The need to provide adequate customer education must start with customers' specific viewpoints. Their perspectives are defined according to any of the following factors:

Important Issues and Concerns

All too often, salespeople assume that what is important to them is also important to their customers. Properly qualifying customers early in the sales process makes it far easier to understand what is important to them, what they are interested in and what their specific "hot-button" issues are. These are all critical aspects of defining and determining the specific information that needs to be provided.

Needed Information

Once salespeople have completed the qualification process and determined the needs of their customers, they can then begin to define their matched informational requirements. In this manner, it will best suit what they are interested in hearing and learning. When salespeople successfully accomplish this, they maintain and sustain their customers' interest. This allows salespeople to ignite a fire from the spark of interest they originally created in their initial sales calls.

Information to Be Ignored

There is a natural tendency to overwhelm customers with marketing materials, reports, articles, pamphlets and other kinds of referenced documentation. Astute salespeople will understand the information that is needed and review that which is available in order to determine what can be ignored or skimmed within their sales presentations.

The proper filtering of information allows salespeople to create the right balance and make precise presentations in regard to solutions, products and services, without overwhelming customers with data they have little or no use for.

Expertise and Experience

Salespeople should understand the value of their experience when it comes to educating their customers. The application of their know-how adds specific value that competitors will find difficult to replicate. Indeed, the best source of customer education comes from the expertise salespeople have developed over time. Properly done, this can provide the differentiation needed to secure more sales and generate higher levels of customer satisfaction.

There are a number of problems and pitfalls most salespeople can easily and unknowingly stumble into while determining their customers' informational needs, including:

False Assumptions

At the inception of the sales process, many salespeople will make faulty assumptions about the breadth and scope of their customers' knowledge and expertise. These assumptions provide them the justification to skip steps and short-circuit the entire sales process. They see no reason to devote valuable time and energy to properly educating their customers in the inherent value of their products and services and why they represent the best available option.

Information Overload

A common tendency is to overload customers with product brochures, tech specification sheets and other marketing information. These tend to overwhelm them with too much data to include in their product evaluations. In today's hectic business environment, many customers do not have the time to wade through mountains of data and information in order to make informed buying decisions. Additionally, much of the information that is provided often tends to be "marketing hype" that does not address their specific informational needs and concerns.

Failure to Provide Information and Expertise from the Customer's Perspective

In many situations, salespeople are selling their products or services from their own personal point of view and not that of their customers. While the product information and data they provide—often prepackaged marketing material—can be helpful, it often fails to address the specific needs, concerns and problems that must be discussed before a low risk, informed buying decision can be made.

Provide Information and Not Expertise

The reality in today's marketplace is that many customers are drowning in information, yet starving for expertise. Astute salespeople realize this and take the time to distill their information and data down into the expertise their customers need to make better analyzed and informed buying decisions. The value of this expertise is often the differentiating factor in being able to move the process along to a successful close.

Failure to Clarify the Value

Many salespeople fail to manage and control the sales landscape on which they are dealing. This landscape is often defined during the qualifying process, wherein salespeople learn the wants, needs and concerns of their customers. Once these are defined, they need to carefully define and clarify the value of their products and services accordingly. If salespeople fall short in controlling the sales landscape, they allow their customers to easily assume a default position, which is to evaluate all products and services on the basis of their price. It is only through adequate information and expertise that salespeople can move their customers away from this default position.

Too Little Information

There are instances where salespeople become too measured in the delivery of their information and expertise. Whatever the reason—inexperience or simple laziness—the lack of adequate information and expertise does not provide customers with sufficient knowledge to make informed, low risk buying decisions. As aforementioned, when this occurs customers automatically default to the lowest price as the basis for making their final purchasing decisions.

POINTS TO PONDER – SOMETHING TO THINK ABOUT

1. Do you understand that the failure to fully educate your customers concerning your products and services increases the purchasing risk in their minds?
2. Do you understand that the failure to inform your customers in regard to your product or service value undermines your ability to effectively sell to them?
3. How do you use your expertise and experience to your personal advantage within the sales process?
4. How closely do you pay attention to your customers' perspectives?

TRAINING ACTIVITY — APPLICATION & ACTION PLAN

1. Review the following list:
   - Faulty Assumptions
   - Information Overload
   - Failure to Provide Information and Expertise from the Customer's Perspective
   - Provide Information and Not Expertise
   - Failure to Clarify the Value
   - Too Little Information
2. Evaluate your sales performance against your ability to adequately educate your customers.
3. Review the list and determine which of the items you are most guilty of using.
4. Develop specific sales strategies that allow you to overcome these deficiencies in order to adequately educate your customers.

8

Why Product Knowledge Offers Competitive Advantage

Many companies will focus attention on product training in an effort to develop adequate product knowledge within their sales team. While intentions are often good, it is the implementation of this training that often goes awry. Adequate product knowledge must be linked with specific sales skills in order to create the competitive advantage these companies are seeking.

Sales problems that are caused by inadequate product knowledge are easily resolved. Salespeople simply need to provide additional information, expertise and knowledge that helps customers facilitate their decision making regarding their purchases. The key lies in being able to recognize the various symptoms and signs indicating clients require additional information.

IMPLICATIONS — WHAT THIS MEANS TO YOU

The dissemination of product information is often the focus of many salespeople. They will highlight the features and benefits of specific products and services they feel their customers need. The problem is that many buyers are overwhelmed with information and starving for expertise and knowledge that they require to make successful business decisions. Many salespeople fall down in making the transition from imparting information to knowledge. They lack the skills and expertise to make this shift and successfully garner the sale.

Customers have an increasingly large number of choices available to them when making a buying decision. More importantly, all competitors are making similar claims about the results their products or services are able to produce. Consequently, it is becoming increasingly difficult for salespeople to rise above the competitive din to create the space they require to obtain a selling advantage. Salespeople must know how to specifically create a competitive advantage for themselves through the specific application of product knowledge.

Salespeople who solely focus their product knowledge around features and benefits are only communicating a part of the story to their customers. They are not adequately defining the value that their product offers or the reasons why customers should buy from them. Consequently, they are providing insufficient information, knowledge and expertise that customers require to make an informed decision.

It is important for salespeople to appreciate that it is their responsibility to both demonstrate the unique value their products and services offer their customers and educate them as to why what they are offering represents their best available option. Anything less communicates an incomplete message and fails to provide customers with adequate reasons to buy.

STRATEGIES, TIPS & TECHNIQUES TO APPLY

Many salespeople will actually minimize the value of their products and services by directly linking them to the features and benefits offered by competitors' products and services. These salespeople feel their position is enhanced by communicating a message to their customers that their products are exactly like those of their competitors. This is especially true if there is a well-known brand name that salespeople are competing against.

What they fail to understand is that by doing this, they completely undermine both their sales message and position and actually provide customers the reasons to purchase the competitors' offerings. These salespeople have either insufficient knowledge or information about their products, or they fail to understand why their offerings are unique and have to clearly differentiate and position them against the competition. There is a strong correlation between product differentiation, product space and overall value, and it is up to salespeople to link these three factors together in order to successfully position themselves and communicate a strong sales message.

Product Differentiation

If all salespeople are selling the same products and offering the same results to customers, then obviously other factors must be considered when making a buying decision. These factors may include service, price, customer relationship, reputation and a host of other variables that impact the buying decision. If they want to spark their customers' interest and motivate and energize them to move forward in the sales process, salespeople must be able to completely differentiate themselves from their competition from the start.

Salespeople who experience high levels of customer brush-offs and objections early in the sales process are suffering from an inability to differentiate themselves from the competition. When this occurs with regularity, salespeople have to question their initial approach to customers and specifically identify information and factors that clearly differentiates themselves from the competition and at the same time sparks their customers' interest.

Product Space

When salespeople are able to differentiate both their products and services from those of the competition, they are in fact defining the product space between them. The wider the product space between their products and competitive offerings, the better salespeople are able to position themselves in the minds of their customers. A failure to clearly delineate the product space will result in an increasing number of objections and pricing issues during the sales process. These normally will surface midway through the process and persist as salespeople push to close the sale.

Salespeople must understand that major sales often hinge on minor product differences, especially when the product space is extremely close and there are few features that differentiate one product from another. Most customers base their buying decisions on differences, whether real or perceived. Therefore, in many situations where products and services are similar, it is up to salespeople to create perceived differences within the customer's mind. The ultimate success of the sale will depend on how well salespeople position themselves in the customer's mind and create real or perceived differences between their products and services.

Product Value

Clearly presenting product difference and product space establishes value in the mind of the buyer. Failure to create distinct value in the customer's mind relegates products and services to commodity status. When this occurs, customers who cannot clearly differentiate one product from another will automatically default to the lowest price or other distinguishing factors, and salespeople will see an increase in price objections, stalls and other forms of objections that will keep them from moving forward. It is up to salespeople to clearly define their product's or service's value within customers' minds. As with product differences, these values can either be real or perceived. It will all depend upon how salespeople are able to convey these values in both tangible and intangible terms.

Salespeople must employ specific strategies and techniques in order to prevent customers from making decisions on the basis of price alone and create a competitive advantage for themselves. These include:

Similar Products

As the inability to create a distinction between similar products is a major problem for many salespeople, it is essential that they develop expertise not only in their own products and services, but also in those offered by their competitors. Only when salespeople acquire this expertise can they intimately know the differences between competitive products and services. Knowledge of these product intricacies gives salespeople the expertise to link minor but critical differences to the specific needs of their customers—and a leg up on the competition.

Similar Claims

When salespeople are competing against like products and services, it is not uncommon to have to deal with similar claims. When this occurs, salespeople must isolate their experiences and know how to counter specific competitive claims of results that can be achieved using their products. While at first blush many competitive claims will appear similar, it is only upon in-depth analysis that salespeople are able to refute or differentiate between claims based upon the duration, durability, reputation, value and other factors impacting the results provided by one product or another.

Salespeople need to dissect competitive claims with a point-by-point analysis in order to highlight the critical features offered by their products and services alone. They should not deny these claims during appointments and appear to attack the competition, but focus the customer's attention on the critical differences and results their products or services offer over other vendors.

False or Misleading Claims

Even when salespeople have unique and innovative products or services, it is not uncommon to hear customers relate that competitors are making similar and often inaccurate claims about the results their products or services can produce. This often places salespeople in a defensive position as they try to differentiate their products and counter or refute such claims. It creates a perception in customers' minds that the salesperson is suffering from a case of "sour grapes."

What, in fact, has occurred is that the competitor, fully understanding their product and competitive weaknesses, has muddied the waters with false and deceptive claims and created confusion within the marketplace. Competitors are hoping to benefit from this confusion, using it to overcome their own weaknesses.

Rather than attempting to directly refute false and deceptive competitive claims, salespeople are better served to create distinct product space and verify the specific results of their own offering. One technique involves highlighting specific results and then asking customers whether competitors are able to document and match them. This allows salespeople to strengthen their position while leading customers to question the veracity of such competitive claims.

Default to the Lowest Price

When customers automatically default in their decision making to the lowest available price, this indicates that either the customer is confused, or the salesperson has not sufficiently established and clarified the value of their offering. When customers have not been adequately educated as to the best option available to them, salespeople need to focus on value and quantify the features and benefits offered by their products and services through value analysis. It is essential for salespeople to quantify each tangible and intangible factor that is impacted by their products and services and demonstrate their value to customers. The use of specific quantitative analysis tools allows salespeople to create a compelling and demonstrable competitive advantage for their products and services.

POINTS TO PONDER — SOMETHING TO THINK ABOUT

1. Have you considered stalls and customer objections to be veiled requests for further information and clarification?
2. How effectively are you able to wield information, knowledge and expertise in order to build an effective sales argument that results in sales?
3. What techniques do you use to establish competitive advantage in a market place that is cluttered with similar products?
4. How frequently do you observe customers automatically defaulting to the lowest price in their decision making?

TRAINING ACTIVITY — APPLICATION & ACTION PLAN

1. Identify specific sales experiences with the following:
    - Similar Products
    - Similar Claims
    - False or Misleading Claims
    - Default to the Lowest Price
2. Analyze each example and situation that you have selected to determine specifically what occurred and the exact reasons why.
3. Identify the specific lessons learned from your analysis.
4. Determine how to apply these lessons to future sales situations.

About the Author

Timothy F. Bednarz, Ph.D. is CEO of the American Management Development Group, Inc. For over 20 years he has researched, designed and authored hundreds of learning and development programs used by Fortune 1000 companies.

He is also the author of *Great! What Makes Leaders Great. What They Did, How They Did It and What You Can Learn from It* (2011).

Speaking Availability

Timothy F. Bednarz, Ph.D. is available for speaking engagements for your next meeting or association event. He can be contacted at 800-654-4935 or by e-mail at timothy.bednarz@majorium.com.

Bulk Sales

Bulk sales of this book or any other titles available from Majorium Business Press. Inquiries can be directed to sales@majorium.com, or by phone at 800-6654-4935.

Quick Order Form

Fax orders: 715-342-1118. Send this form.

Telephone orders: Call 800-654-4935 toll-free. Have your credit card ready.

Email orders: sales@majorium.com

Postal orders: Majorium Business Press, 2025 Main Street, Stevens Point, WI 54481, USA.

Please send the following books:

____

____

____

____

Please send more FREE information on:

❑Catalog ❑Speaking/Seminars ❑Mailing Lists ❑Consulting

Name: ____

Address: ____

City: _____________________________ State: _____ Zip: __________

Telephone: ____

Email address: ____

Sales tax: Please add 5.5% for products shipped to Wisconsin addresses.

Shipping by air:

United States: $4.00 for first book and $2.00 for each additional product.

International: $9.00 for first book; $5.00 for each additional product (estimate).

Made in United States
Orlando, FL
04 November 2026

90202053R00037